Discovering India

Jo Chambers

Contents

India's States   2

Getting Around   4

Sights   6

Life in India   8

Religions   10

Food   12

Going to the Movies   14

Sum It Up   16

India is a huge country with different states. Estimate, then count the number of states on the map.

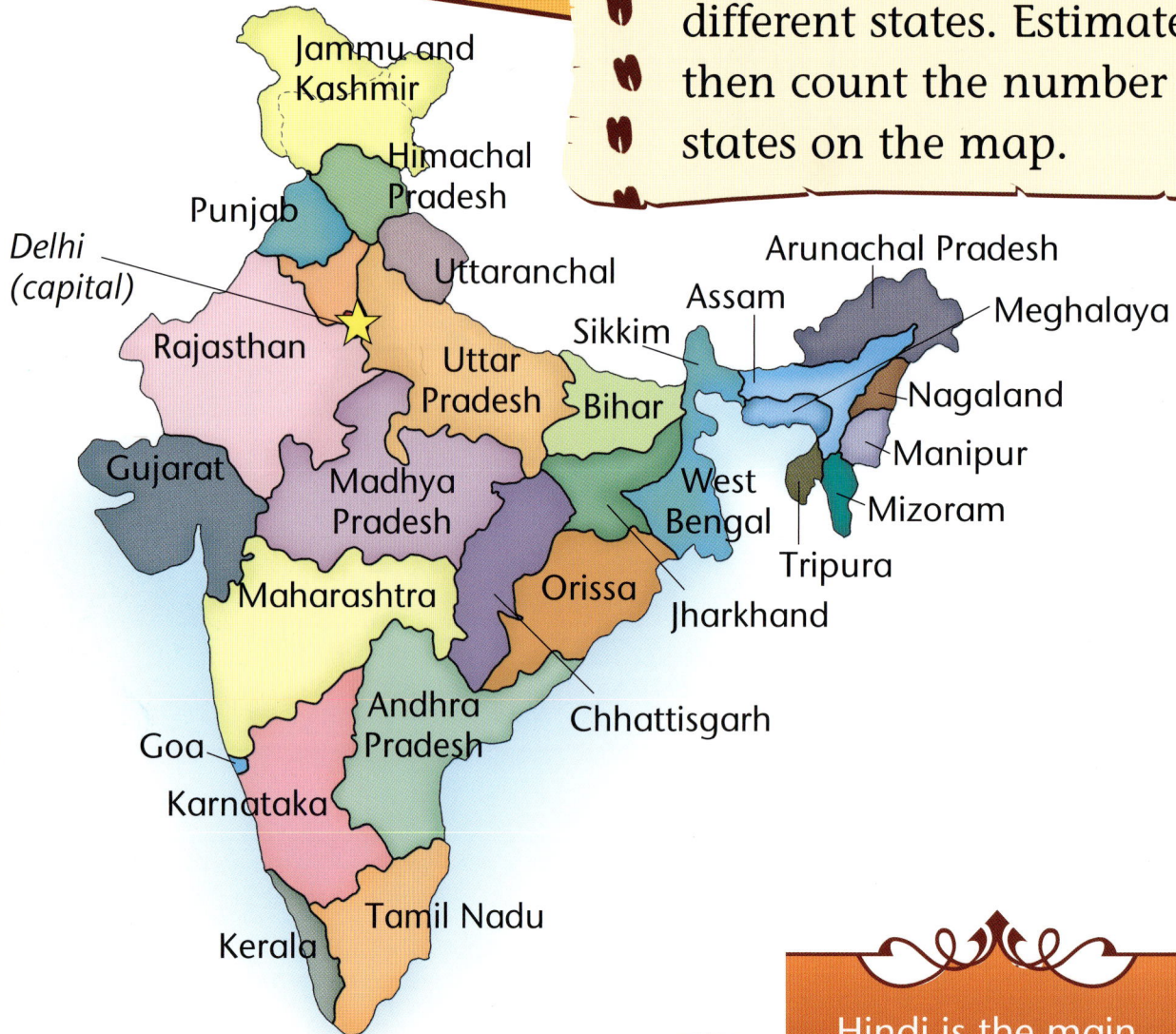

Jammu and Kashmir

Himachal Pradesh

Punjab

Delhi (capital)

Uttaranchal

Arunachal Pradesh

Assam

Meghalaya

Rajasthan

Sikkim

Nagaland

Uttar Pradesh

Bihar

Manipur

Gujarat

Mizoram

Madhya Pradesh

West Bengal

Tripura

Maharashtra

Orissa

Jharkhand

Andhra Pradesh

Chhattisgarh

Goa

Karnataka

Tamil Nadu

Kerala

A traveler visits 12 states in 1 trip. How many are left to visit next time?

Hindi is the main language in 10 Indian states. How many states have a different main language?

KEY WORDS
- estimate
- left
- subtract
- less
- difference

India has many different kinds of weather, but the monsoon affects the whole country. This brings high temperatures and lots of rain.

Mumbai is in Maharashtra. Which month is the hottest? How many degrees colder is the coldest month? Find the difference in rainfall between June and October.

The weather in Mumbai

Month	Temp (°F/°C)	Rain (in./cm)
January	81/27	0
February	82/28	0
March	86/30	0
April	90/32	0
May	91/33	.8/2
June	90/32	19/48
July	84/29	24/62
August	84/29	13/34
September	84/29	10/26
October	90/32	2/6
November	90/32	.4/1
December	88/31	0

TOOLS

1	2	3	4	5	6	7	8	9	10
11	12	13	14	15	16	17	18	19	20
21	22	23	24	25	26	27	28	29	30
31	32	33	34	35	36	37	38	39	40

3

Getting Around

Many kinds of transportation are used in India. Count the different vehicles. Are there more cars or train cars in this picture?

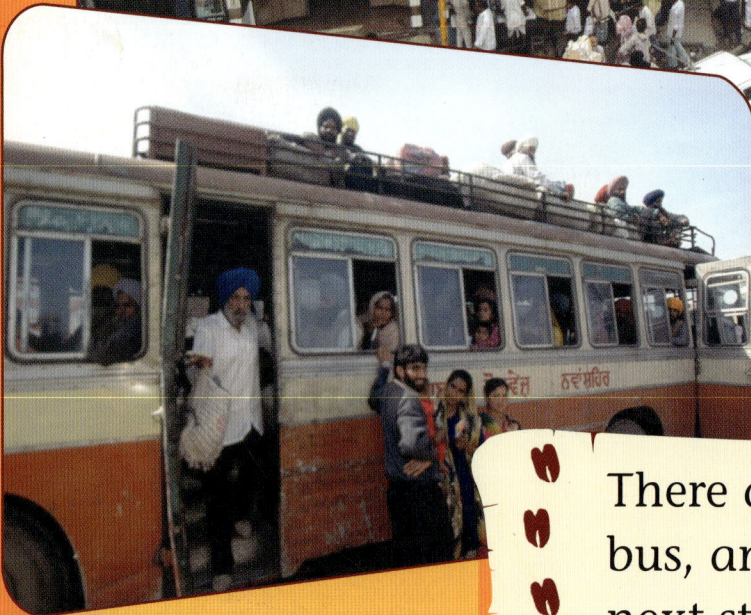

There are 18 people on this bus, and 6 get off at the next stop. How many people are left on the bus?

Trains are very popular. People travel inside and on the roof.

FACT!

Indian railways move 10 million passengers a day along 38,525 miles (62,000 km) of track.

On this train, 3 more people get on the roof. Now how many are riding on the roof?

Find different ways of having 10 people on one car, with some on the roof and some inside.

TOOLS

1	2	3	4	5	6	7	8	9	10
11	12	13	14	15	16	17	18	19	20
21	22	23	24	25	26	27	28	29	30

Sights

This is the Taj Mahal. How many domes can you see? If the minarets fell down how many other domes would be left?

FACT! It took 20,000 workers 22 years to build the Taj Mahal.

Dome

Minaret

The Golden Temple is where the Sikh holy book is kept. Sikhs come to see the book and bathe in the holy waters.

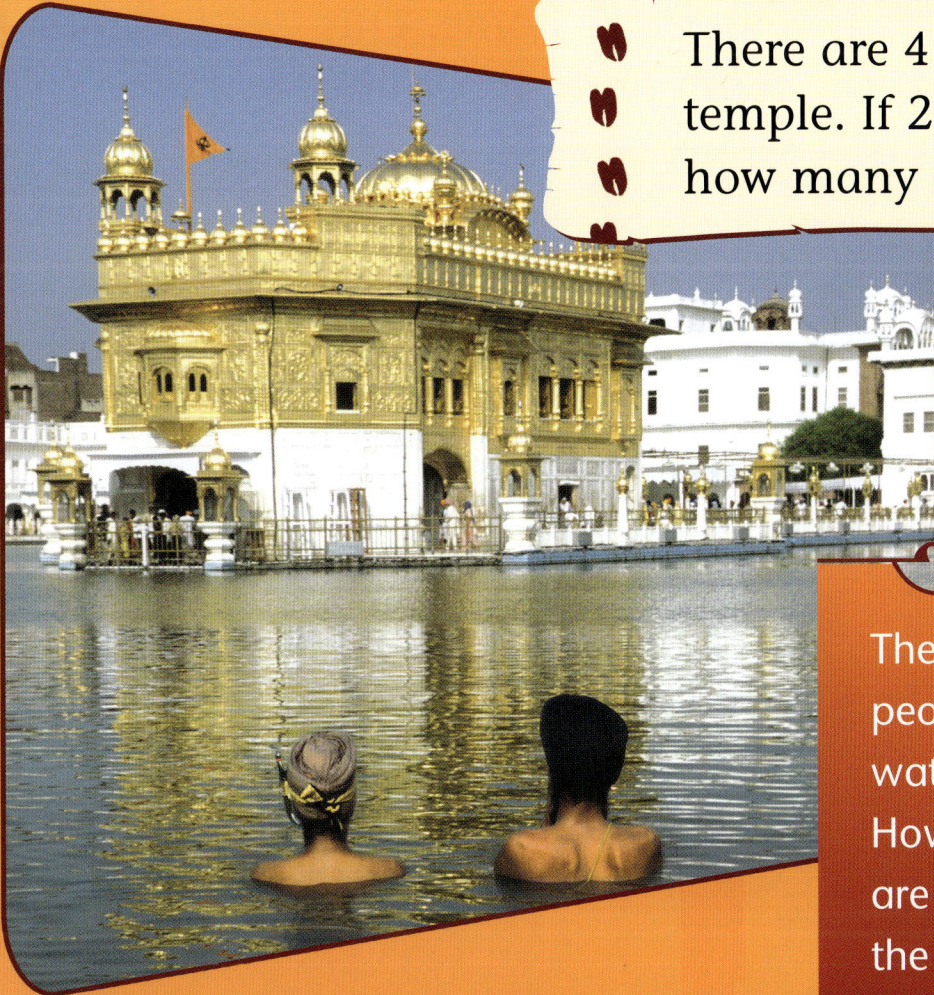

There are 4 doors into the temple. If 2 are closed, how many are left open?

There are 16 people in the water altogether. How many people are not shown in the photo?

TOOLS

1	2	3	4	5	6	7	8
9	10	11	12	13	14	15	16

Life in India

In India, many family members live together in 1 home. This is very common in the villages.

More than 1 billion people live in India.

Are there more children or adults in the picture? How many more children are there than adults?

Some people leave the villages and move to the cities to look for work. Often, they live in shantytowns at the edge of the cities.

KEY WORDS

- more
- fewest
- difference
- how many left?

Many people moved from Nanga village to the city. How many are left in the village?

Nanga Village		
Family	Number in family	Number who moved to the city
Family Bharti	8	3
Family Singh	10	5
Family Khan	9	4
Family Kapoor	7	2

Which family had the fewest members move to the city? What do you notice about the numbers left in the village?

TOOLS

0 1 2 3 4 5 6 7 8 9 10 11 12

Religions

Hinduism and Buddhism are two of the religions practiced in India.

Hindu families worship in temples.

Each family has 8 members, but some have gone to the temple. How many have gone from each family?

Find the difference between the total number at the temple and the total who have stayed at home.

KEY WORDS

- difference
- how many have gone?
- how many left?
- less
- fewer

Buddhists believe that Buddha found enlightenment while sitting under the Bo tree. Now Buddhists tie prayer flags near the Bo tree.

The blue flags are taken away. How many flags are left?

Imagine there are 2 lines with 12 flags altogether. One line has 2 fewer flags than the other. How many flags are on each line?

TOOLS

0 1 2 3 4 5 6 7 8 9 10 11 12

Food

Haats are open-air markets where fruits, vegetables, grains, spices, and many other items are sold. They are colorful, noisy places.

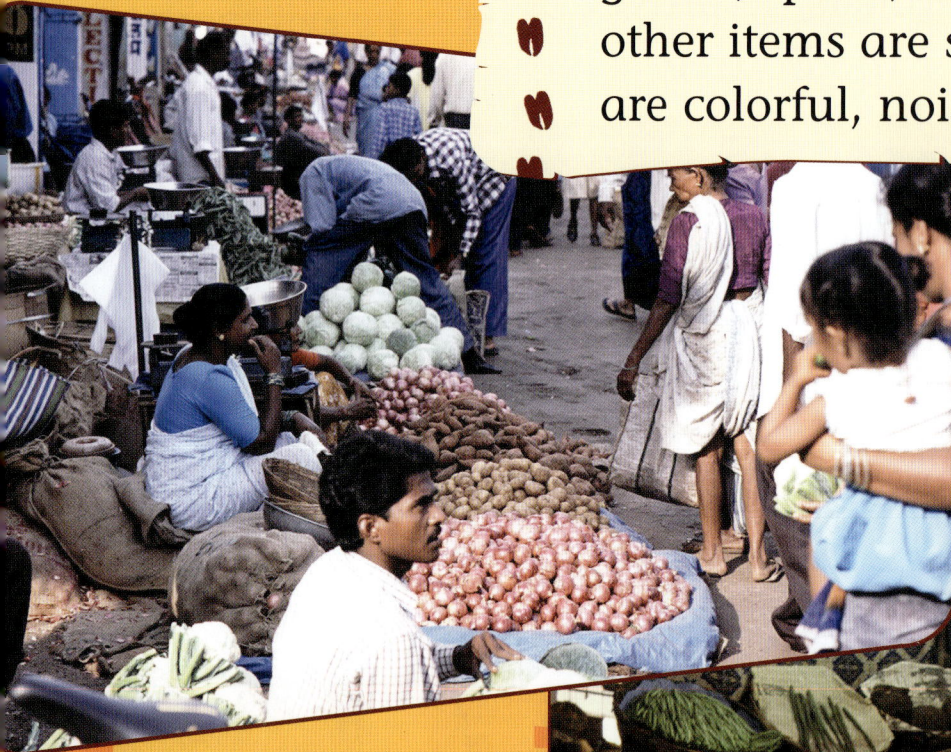

This man is buying 6 vegetables. He has chosen 1 vegetable. How many more does he need?

Spices have a strong smell. They are used in cooking to flavor food.

Onion Bhaji

4 onions
1 cup of vinegar
1 cup of flour
2 teaspoons of cumin powder
1 teaspoon of turmeric
1 teaspoon of chili powder
1 teaspoon of salt
1 cup of vegetable oil

KEY WORDS

- how many?
- how much?
- how many more?
- left

How many spices are used in this recipe?

FACT!

An onion bhaji weighing nearly 132 pounds (60 kg) and measuring 32 inches (80 cm) across was made in Yorkshire, England, in 1999.

The cumin, turmeric, chili, and salt are mixed together. How many teaspoons of ingredients is this? Next, 3 teaspoons of this mixture are added to the onions. How much of the mixture is left?

The recipe is for 4 people. How much flour would be needed for 8 people?

TOOLS

| 1 | 2 | 3 | 4 | 5 | 6 | 7 | 8 | 9 | 10 |

Going to the Movies

Going to the movies is a favorite treat for Indian families and friends. Estimate the number of people waiting to go into this theater.

FACT!

India is the world's largest movie producer, making more than 2 times as many movies as the USA.

PARKING

TEA, COFFEE & SNACKS

TIGER EYES ★★★

TICKETS
Adult: 7 Rupees

Here, 12 people want to see *Tiger Eyes* and 3 fewer want to see *Lost Prince*. How many is that? How many people are watching these 2 movies altogether?

What is the cost of 1 adult and 1 child ticket together? How much more is 1 adult ticket than 1 child ticket?

If a person has 10 rupees, and buys 1 adult ticket, how many rupees will be left?

How many adult tickets can be bought with 20 rupees?

LOST PRINCE ★ ★ ★

TICKETS
Child: 4 Rupees

TOOLS

1	2	3	4	5	6	7	8	9	10
11	12	13	14	15	16	17	18	19	20

15

Sum It Up

This train is very crowded. At the next station, 3 of the men standing in the doorway get off. How many are still in the doorway?

There were 18 treats on the banana leaf. How many have been eaten?

Each man in the train doorway takes 1 of the treats shown on the leaf. How many treats are left?

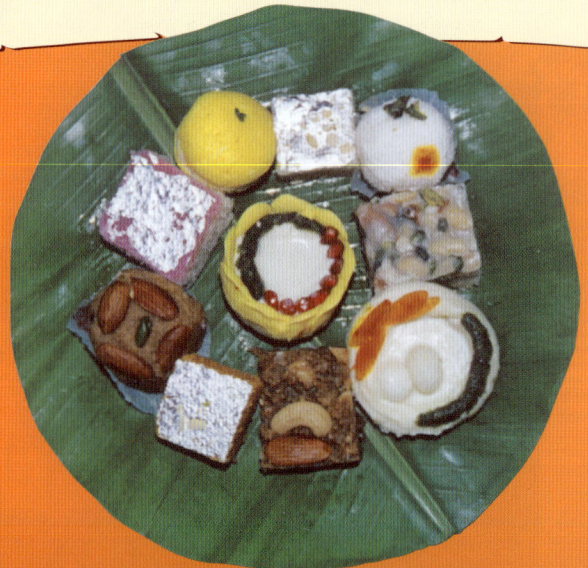